General Instruction

Project Note

Additional materials will be listed with each project.

Instructions

1 Cut and stitch plastic canvas following instructions for each purse.

2 For handles, cut a 12-inch length flexible bead stringing wire for each purse. Thread wire down through one hole indicated on right side of purse top and up through adjacent hole indicated. Thread on a crimp bead over both strands, leaving about a 1-inch tail, then crimp bead next to purse top.

3 Using beads desired, determine bead pattern and length of handle desired. *Note: Each handle should have a center bead with bead pattern same on both sides of center bead.* Thread on beads, making sure to thread first few beads over both strands.

4 Add remaining crimp bead to wire, then thread wire through holes on left side of purse top following instructions in step 2. Thread end of wire through a few beads, then pull up wire so there is no space between beads. Crimp bead and trim any wire ends.

Materials

Each Purse

❏ Uniek Needloft plastic canvas yarn as listed in color key
❏ #16 tapestry needle
❏ 2 small silver chain crimps #31903 from Blue Moon Beads
❏ 12 inches Beadalon .015-inch flexible bead stringing wire
❏ Wire cutters
❏ Needle-nose pliers or crimpers
❏ Hot-glue gun
❏ 3-inch square sticky-note memo pad

Leopard Purse

Size: 3¾ inches W x 3⅝ inches H x ¾ inch D
(9.5cm x 9.2cm x 1.9cm), excluding handle
and button

Skill Level: Beginner

Materials

❏ ½ sheet 7-count plastic canvas
❏ Assorted Czech glass beads from Blue Moon
Beads Bead Mix Jet #32433
❏ 2 (3⅝ inches/9.2cm) lengths black fringe

Stitching Step by Step

1 Cut plastic canvas according to graphs.

2 Stitch front, back and top as graphed, working uncoded areas with camel Continental Stitches. Do not stitch inside pocket.

3 Using camel throughout, Whipstitch front and back to top. Place inside pocket on wrong side of back where indicated with brackets. Overcast around edges of assembled purse, Whipstitching pocket in place along side and bottom edges of back while Overcasting.

4 Following general instructions, assemble handle. Glue one length fringe each to front and back along top edges.

5 Slide last few pages of memo pad inside pocket.

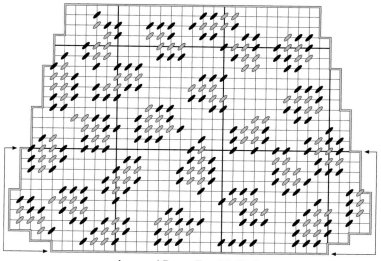

Leopard Purse Front & Back
34 holes x 24 holes
Cut 2

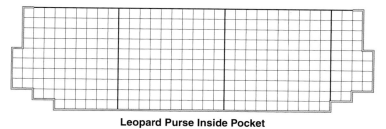

Leopard Purse Inside Pocket
34 holes x 10 holes
Cut 1
Do not stitch

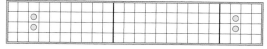

Leopard Purse Top
24 holes x 4 holes
Cut 1

COLOR KEY	
Yards	**Plastic Canvas Yarn**
6 (5.5m)	■ Black #00
6 (5.5m)	▨ Rust #09
16 (14.7m)	Uncoded areas are camel #43 Continental Stitches
	⁄ Camel #43 Overcasting and Whipstitching
	○ Attach handle

Color numbers given are for Uniek Needloft plastic canvas yarn.

Zebra Stripes

Size: 3¾ inches W x 3⅝ inches H x ¾ inch D
(9.5cm x 9.2cm x 1.9cm), excluding handle
and button
Skill Level: Beginner

Materials
❑ ½ sheet 7-count plastic canvas
❑ Assorted Czech glass beads from Blue Moon Beads
glass Bead Mix Jet #32433
❑ ⅞-inch/2.2cm black button

Stitching Step by Step

1 Cut plastic canvas according to graphs. Cut one 24-hole x 10-hole piece for inside pocket. Pocket will remain unstitched.

2 Stitch front, back and top following graphs.

3 Using watermelon throughout, Whipstitch front and back to top. Place pocket on wrong side of back where indicated with brackets. Overcast around edges of assembled purse, Whipstitching pocket in place along side and bottom edges of back while Overcasting.

4 Following general instructions, assemble handle. Glue or sew button to front where indicated.

5 Slide last few pages of memo pad inside pocket

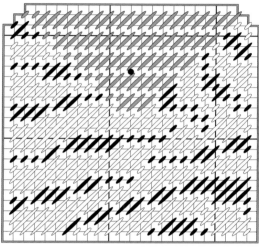

Zebra Stripes Front
24 holes x 23 holes
Cut 1

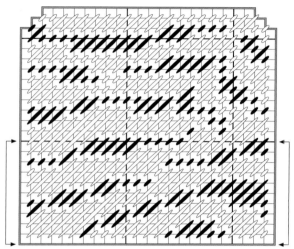

Zebra Stripes Back
24 holes x 23 holes
Cut 1

Zebra Stripes Top
20 holes x 4 holes
Cut 1

COLOR KEY	
Yards	**Plastic Canvas Yarn**
10 (9.2m)	■ Black #00
10 (9.2m)	☐ White #41
8 (7.4m)	▨ Watermelon #55
	○ Attach handle
	● Attach button

Color numbers given are for Uniek Needloft plastic canvas yarn.

Flowers

Size: 3½ inches W x 3½ inches H x ¾ inch D
(8.9cm x 8.9cm x 1.9cm), excluding handle
Skill Level: Beginner

Materials

❏ ½ sheet 7-count plastic canvas
❏ Assorted Czech glass beads from Blue Moon
Beads Bead Mix Summer Splash #35783 and Bead
Mix Sea Breeze #35843

Stitching Step by Step

1 Cut plastic canvas according to graphs. Cut one 23-hole by 10-hole piece for inside pocket. Inside pocket will remain unstitched.

2 Stitch pieces following graphs, working uncoded areas with yellow Continental Stitches.

3 Using yellow throughout, Whipstitch front and back to top. Place inside pocket on wrong side of back where indicated with brackets. Overcast around edges of assembled purse, Whipstitching pocket in place along side and bottom edges of back while Overcasting.

4 Following general instructions, assemble handle using coordinating beads from both bead mixes.

5 Slide last few pages of memo pad inside pocket.

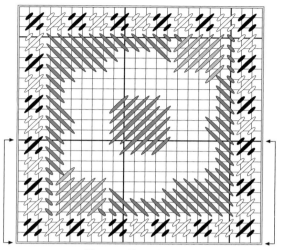

Flowers Front & Back
23 holes x 23 holes
Cut 2

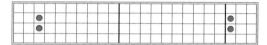

Flowers Top
23 holes x 4 holes
Cut 1

COLOR KEY	
Yards	**Plastic Canvas Yarn**
6 (5.5m)	■ Black #00
2 (1.9m)	▨ Fern #23
4 (3.7m)	▨ Royal #32
6 (5.5m)	☐ White #41
2 (1.9m)	▨ Bright purple #64
10 (9.2m)	Uncoded areas are yellow #57 Continental Stitches
	╱ Yellow #57 Overcasting and Whipstitching
	● Attach handle

Color numbers given are for Uniek Needloft plastic canvas yarn.

Hearts

Size: 3¾ inches W x 3⅝ inches H x ¾ inch D
(9.5cm x 9.2cm x 1.9cm), excluding handle
Skill Level: Beginner

Materials

❏ ½ sheet 7-count plastic canvas
❏ Assorted sizes glass pony beads in colors to coordinate with yarn

Stitching Step by Step

1 Cut plastic canvas according to graphs. Cut one 24-hole x 10-hole piece for inside pocket. Pocket will remain unstitched.

2 Stitch front, back and top following graphs, working uncoded areas with white Continental Stitches.

3 Using turquoise throughout, Whipstitch front and back to top. Place pocket on wrong side of back where indicated with brackets. Overcast around edges of assembled purse, Whipstitching pocket in place along side and bottom edges of back while Overcasting.

4 Following general instructions, assemble handle.

5 Slide last few pages of memo pad inside pocket.

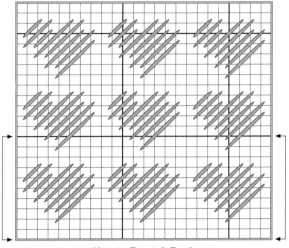

Hearts Front & Back
24 holes x 23 holes
Cut 2

Hearts Top
24 holes x 4 holes
Cut 1

COLOR KEY		
Yards	**Plastic Canvas Yarn**	
12 (11m)	☐ White #41	
10 (9.2m)	▩ Bright orange #58	
	Uncoded areas are white #41 Continental Stitches	
4 (3.7m)	⟋ Turquoise #54 Overcasting and Whipstitching	
	○ Attach handle	

Color numbers given are for Uniek Needloft plastic canvas yarn.

Diagonal Stripes

Size: 3⅞ inches W x 4 inches H x ¾ inch D
(9.8cm x 10.2cm x 1.9cm), excluding handle
and fringe
Skill Level: Beginner

Materials

❏ ½ sheet 7-count plastic canvas
❏ Assorted beads from Blue Moon Beads
   Lampworked Glass Bead Mix green #47044
❏ 24 inches/61cm black fringe

Stitching Step by Step

1 Cut plastic canvas according to graphs. Cut one 25-hole x 10-hole piece for inside pocket. Inside pocket will remain unstitched.

2 Stitch front, back and top, following graphs.

3 Using mermaid throughout, Whipstitch front and back to top. Place inside pocket on wrong side of back where indicated with brackets. Overcast around edges of assembled purse, Whipstitching pocket in place along side and bottom edges of back while Overcasting.

4 Following general instructions, assemble handle.

5 Cut two lengths fringe to fit along bottom edges of front and back; glue in place on reverse side. Cut remaining fringe in half and glue one each to front and back along red lines, folding ends over to reverse side and trimming as needed.

6 Slide last few pages of memo pad inside pocket.

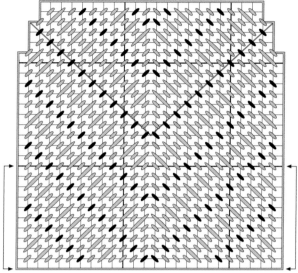

Diagonal Stripes Front & Back
25 holes x 26 holes
Cut 2

Diagonal Stripes Top
21 holes x 4 holes
Cut 1

COLOR KEY	
Yards	**Plastic Canvas Yarn**
8 (7.4m)	■ Black #00
8 (7.4m)	▦ Pumpkin #12
20 (18.3m)	▦ Mermaid #53
	○ Attach handle
Color numbers given are for Uniek Needloft plastic canvas yarn.	

Stripes

Size: 5½ inches W x 3⅝ inches H x ¾ inch D
(14cm x 9.2cm x 1.9cm), excluding handle
and button

Skill Level: Beginner

Materials

❏ ½ sheet 7-count plastic canvas
❏ Assorted Czech glass beads from Blue Moon
Beads Bead Mix Summer Splash #35783
❏ 1 large yellow and white flower button

Stitching Step by Step

1 Cut plastic canvas according to graphs.

2 Stitch front and top as graphed, working uncoded
areas with turquoise Continental Stitches; work back
with stripe pattern only. Do not stitch inside pocket.

3 Using turquoise throughout, Whipstitch front and
back to top. Place inside pocket on wrong side of
back where indicated with brackets. Overcast around
edges of assembled purse, Whipstitching pocket in place
along side and bottom edges of back while Overcasting.

4 Following general instructions, assemble handle.
Glue or sew button to front where indicated.

5 Slide last few pages of memo pad inside pocket.

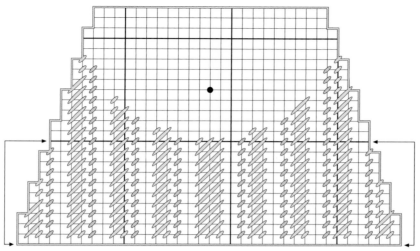

Stripes Front & Back
36 holes x 23 holes
Cut 2
Stitch front as graphed
Stitch back with stripe pattern only

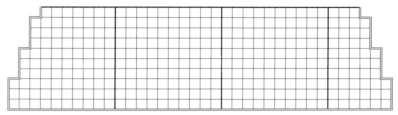

Stripes Inside Pocket
36 holes x 10 holes
Cut 1
Do not stitch

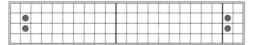

Stripes Top
22 holes x 4 holes
Cut 1

COLOR KEY

Yards	Plastic Canvas Yarn
7 (6.5m)	☐ Fern #23
10 (9.2m)	☐ Yellow #57
10 (9.2m)	Uncoded areas are turquoise #54 Continental Stitches
	⁄ Turquoise #54 Overcasting and Whipstitching
	● Attach handle
	● Attach button

Color numbers given are for Uniek Needloft plastic canvas yarn.

Plaid Purse

Size: 4⅛ inches W x 3½ inches H x ¾ inch D
(10.5cm x 8.9cm x 1.9cm), excluding handle
and buttons

Skill Level: Beginner

Materials

❏ ½ sheet 7-count plastic canvas
❏ Assorted Czech glass beads from Blue Moon
    Beads Bead Mix Gold #32393
❏ 2 (½-inch/1.3cm) yellow buttons

Stitching Step by Step

1 Cut plastic canvas according to graphs. Cut one 27-hole by 10-hole piece for inside pocket. Inside pocket will remain unstitched.

2 Stitch and Overcast tabs following graphs. Stitch front, back and top pieces.

3 Using watermelon throughout, Whipstitch front and back to top. Place inside pocket on wrong side of back where indicated with brackets. Overcast around edges of assembled purse, Whipstitching pocket in place along side and bottom edges of back while Overcasting.

4 Following general instructions, assemble handle. Center buttons on tabs; glue or sew in place. Glue tabs to front and back where highlighted with blue.

5 Slide last few pages of memo pad inside pocket.

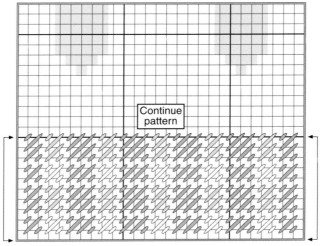

Plaid Purse Front & Back
27 holes x 23 holes
Cut 2

Continue pattern

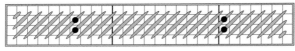

Plaid Purse Top
27 holes x 4 holes
Cut 1

Plaid Purse Tab
5 holes x 7 holes
Cut 2

COLOR KEY	
Yards	**Plastic Canvas Yarn**
8 (7.4m)	Pumpkin #12
6 (5.5m)	White #41
15 (13.8m)	Watermelon #55
6 (5.5m)	Yellow #57
	● Attach handle

Color numbers given are for Uniek Needloft plastic canvas yarn.

Purple Dots

Size: 4⅝ inches W x 3⅜ inches H x ¾ inch D
(11.7cm x 8.6cm x 1.9cm), excluding handle
and cabochon

Skill Level: Beginner

Materials

❏ ½ sheet 7-count plastic canvas
❏ Assorted lampworked glass beads from Blue
Moon Beads Natural Purple Mix #57225 and
Natural Pink Mix #57265
❏ 18mm x 13mm pink oval cabochon

Stitching Step by Step

1 Cut plastic canvas according to graphs.

2 Stitch front, back and top as graphed, working uncoded areas with orchid Continental Stitches. Do not stitch inside pocket.

3 Using purple throughout, Whipstitch front and back to top. Place inside pocket on wrong side of back where indicated with brackets. Overcast around edges of assembled purse, Whipstitching pocket in place along side and bottom edges of back while Overcasting.

4 Following general instructions, assemble handle using coordinating beads from both bead mixes. Center and glue cabochon to top.

5 Slide last few pages of memo pad inside pocket.

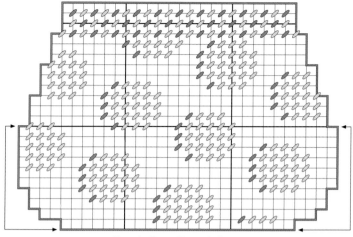

Purple Dots Front & Back
30 holes x 22 holes
Cut 2

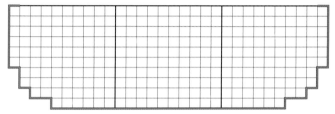

Purple Dots Inside Pocket
30 holes x 10 holes
Cut 1
Do not stitch

Purple Dots Top
22 holes x 4 holes
Cut 1

COLOR KEY	
Yards	**Plastic Canvas Yarn**
8 (7.4m)	☐ Lilac #45
8 (7.4m)	■ Purple #46
9 (8.3m)	Uncoded background is orchid #44 Continental Stitches
	◉ Attach handle
Color numbers given are for Uniek Needloft plastic canvas yarn.	

Stars & Stripes

Size: 4⅛ inches W x 3½ inches H x ¾ inch D
(10.5cm x 8.9cm x 1.9cm), excluding handle
and buttons

Skill Level: Beginner

Materials

❏ ½ sheet 7-count plastic canvas
❏ Assorted Czech glass beads from Blue Moon
Beads Bead Mix Dark Blue #32333
❏ 2 (⅝-inch/1.6cm) white star buttons

Stitching Step by Step

1 Cut plastic canvas according to graphs. Cut one
27-hole by 10-hole piece for inside pocket. Inside
pocket will remain unstitched.

2 Stitch and Overcast front, back and top following
graphs, working uncoded areas with Christmas red
Continental Stitches.

3 Using royal, Whipstitch front and back to top. Place
inside pocket on wrong side of back where indicated
with brackets. Using Christmas red and royal, Overcast
around edges of assembled purse, Whipstitching pocket in
place along side and bottom edges of back while Overcasting.

4 Following general instructions, assemble handle.
Glue or sew buttons in place.

5 Slide last few pages of memo pad inside pocket.

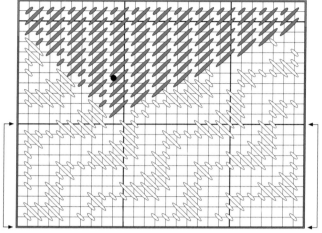

Stars & Stripes Front & Back
27 holes x 22 holes
Cut 2

Stars & Stripes Top
27 holes x 4 holes
Cut 1

COLOR KEY	
Yards	**Plastic Canvas Yarn**
6 (5.5m)	■ Royal #32
6 (5.5m)	□ White #41
8 (7.4m)	Uncoded areas are Christmas red #02 Continental Stitches
	╱ Christmas red #02 Overcasting and Whipstitching
	○ Attach handle
	● Attach button
Color numbers given are for Uniek Needloft plastic canvas yarn.	

Watermelon Bag

Size: 4⅛ inches W x 3¾ inches H x ¾ inch D
(10.5cm x 9.5cm x 1.9cm), excluding handle
and seed-shaped beads

Skill Level: Beginner

Materials

❑ ½ sheet 7-count plastic canvas
❑ Assorted Czech glass beads from Blue Moon Beads
Bead Mix Pink #32373 and Bead Mix Jet #32433
❑ Assorted lampworked glass beads from Blue Moon
Beads Natural Pink Mix #57265

Stitching Step by Step

1 Cut plastic canvas according to graphs.

2 Stitch front, back and top following graphs. Do not stitch inside pocket.

3 Using Christmas green, moss, pink and watermelon, Whipstitch front and back to top.

4 Place inside pocket on wrong side of back where indicated with brackets. Using Christmas green, Overcast around edges of assembled purse, Whipstitching pocket in place along side and bottom edges of back while Overcasting.

5 Following general instructions, assemble handle using coordinating beads from both pink bead mixes. Glue black seed-shaped beads from jet mix on watermelon stitches as desired.

6 Slide last few pages of memo pad inside pocket.

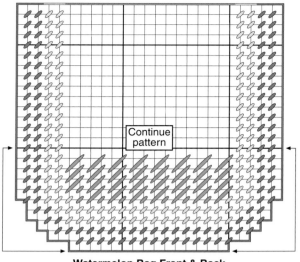

Watermelon Bag Front & Back
25 holes x 24 holes
Cut 2

Continue
pattern

Watermelon Bag Inside Pocket
25 holes x 10 holes
Cut 1
Do not stitch

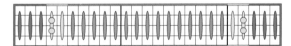

Watermelon Bag Top
25 holes x 4 holes
Cut 1

COLOR KEY	
Yards	**Plastic Canvas Yarn**
4 (3.7m)	☐ Pink #07
4 (3.7m)	☐ Moss #25
10 (9.2m)	■ Christmas green #28
15 (13.8m)	▨ Watermelon #55
	○ Attach handle

Color numbers given are for Uniek
Needloft plastic canvas yarn.

Beach Bag

Size: 4⅝ inches W x 3¾ inches H x ¾ inch D
(11.7cm x 9.5cm x 1.9cm), excluding handle

Skill Level: Beginner

Materials

- ❏ ½ sheet 7-count plastic canvas
- ❏ Lion Brand Fun Fur eyelash yarn as listed in color key
- ❏ Assorted Czech glass beads from Blue Moon Beads Bead Mix Summer Splash #35783

Stitching Step by Step

1 Cut plastic canvas according to graphs.

2 Stitch front, back and top as graphed, working uncoded areas with bright green Continental Stitches. Do not stitch inside pocket.

3 When background stitching is completed, work tangerine eyelash yarn Straight Stitch on both front and back where indicated, gluing on reverse side and tacking or gluing in place on front as needed.

4 Using bright blue throughout, Whipstitch front and back to top. Place inside pocket on wrong side of back where indicated with brackets. Overcast around edges of assembled purse, Whipstitching pocket in place along side and bottom edges of back while Overcasting.

5 Following general instructions, assemble two separate handles where indicated.

6 Slide last few pages of memo pad inside pocket.

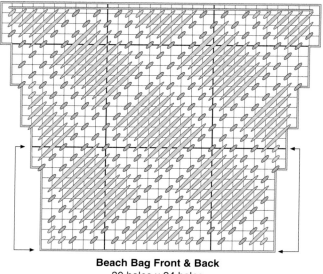

Beach Bag Front & Back
30 holes x 24 holes
Cut 2

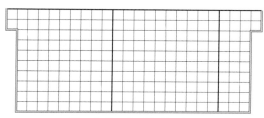

Beach Bag Inside Pocket
24 holes x 10 holes
Cut 1
Do not stitch

Handle 1

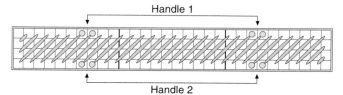

Handle 2
Beach Bag Top
30 holes x 4 holes
Cut 1

COLOR KEY

Yards	Plastic Canvas Yarn
8 (7.4m)	▨ Bright orange #58
20 (18.3m)	☐ Bright blue #60
8 (7.4m)	Uncoded areas are bright green #61 Continental Stitches
	Eyelash Yarn
1 (1m)	⟋ Tangerine #133 Straight Stitch
	◯ Attach handle

Color numbers given are for Uniek Needloft plastic canvas yarn and Lion Brand Yarn Fun Fur eyelash yarn.

Palm Tree Bag

Size: 3⅜ inches W x 3⅞ inches H x ¾ inch D
(8.6cm x 9.8cm x 1.9cm), excluding handle

Skill Level: Beginner

Materials

❏ ½ sheet 7-count plastic canvas
❏ Assorted Czech glass beads from Blue Moon Beads Bead Mix Sea Breeze #35843 and Bead Mix Light Blue #32343
❏ Bright green fur or eyelash yarn

Stitching Step by Step

1 Cut plastic canvas according to graphs. Cut one 22-hole x 10-hole piece for inside pocket. Inside pocket will remain unstitched.

2 Stitch front, back and top, working uncoded areas with bright blue Continental Stitches. Work fern Straight Stitches for beach plants.

3 Using bright blue throughout, Whipstitch front and back to top. Place inside pocket on wrong side of back where indicated with brackets. Overcast around edges of assembled purse, Whipstitching pocket in place along side and bottom edges of back while Overcasting.

4 Following general instructions, assemble handle using coordinating beads from both bead mixes. Glue bright green fur or eyelash yarn to top, covering entire area.

5 Slide last few pages of memo pad inside pocket.

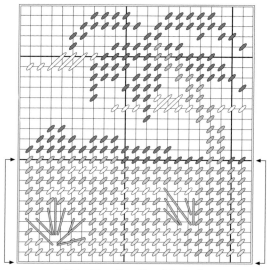

Palm Tree Bag Front & Back
22 holes x 25 holes
Cut 2

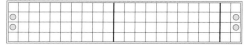

Palm Tree Bag Top
22 holes x 4 holes
Cut 1

COLOR KEY	
Yards	**Plastic Canvas Yarn**
5 (4.6m)	■ Holly #27
2 (1.9m)	□ White #41
3 (2.8m)	▨ Camel #43
2 (1.9m)	■ Dark royal #48
5 (4.6m)	▨ Turquoise #54
2 (1.9m)	□ Pale peach #56
10 (9.2m)	Uncoded areas are bright blue #60 Continental Stitches
	∕ Bright blue #60 Overcasting and Whipstitching
1 (1m)	∕ Fern #23 Straight Stitch
	◯ Attach handle

Color numbers given are for Uniek Needloft plastic canvas yarn.

Envelope Purse

Size: 4⅛ inches W x 3⅜ inches H x ¾ inch D
(10.5cm x 8.6cm x 1.9cm), excluding handle
and button

Skill Level: Beginner

Materials

- ❑ ½ sheet 7-count plastic canvas
- ❑ Assorted Czech glass beads from Blue Moon
  Beads Glass Bead Mix Light Green #32363
- ❑ ⅞-inch/2.2cm green button to match yarn

Stitching Step by Step

1 Cut plastic canvas according to graphs. Cut one 27-hole x 10-hole piece for inside pocket. Pocket will remain unstitched.

2 Stitch front, back and top following graphs.

3 Using black throughout, Whipstitch front and back to top. Place pocket on wrong side of back where indicated with brackets. Overcast around edges of assembled purse, Whipstitching pocket in place along side and bottom edges of back while Overcasting.

4 Following general instructions, assemble handle. Glue or sew button to front where indicated.

5 Slide last few pages of memo pad inside pocket.

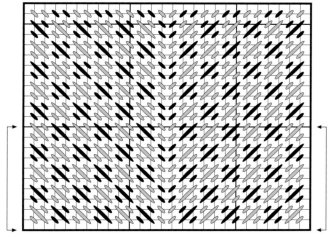

Envelope Purse Back
27 holes x 22 holes
Cut 1

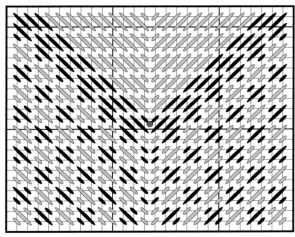

Envelope Purse Front
27 holes x 22 holes
Cut 1

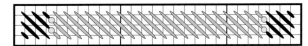

Envelope Purse Top
27 holes x 4 holes
Cut 1

COLOR KEY	
Yards	**Plastic Canvas Yarn**
20 (18.3m)	■ Black #00
10 (9.2m)	▦ Fern #23
	○ Attach handle
	● Attach button

Color numbers given are for Uniek
Needloft plastic canvas yarn.

Red & Purple Purse

Size: 4¾ inches W x 3⅜ inches H x ⅝ inch D
(11.7cm x 8.6cm x 1.6cm), excluding handle
and ornament

Skill Level: Beginner

Materials

❏ ½ sheet 7-count plastic canvas
❏ Assorted beads from Blue Moon Beads
Lampworked Glass Bead Mix Red #47054

Stitching Step by Step

1 Cut plastic canvas according to graphs.

2 Stitch and Overcast ornament following graph. Stitch top, front and back, working front as graphed and back entirely with Christmas red Continental Stitches. Do not stitch inside pocket.

3 Using bright purple, Whipstitch front and back to top.

4 Place inside pocket on wrong side of back where indicated with brackets. Using Christmas red and bright purple, Overcast around edges of assembled purse, Whipstitching pocket in place along side and bottom edges of back while Overcasting.

5 Following general instructions, assemble handle. Glue ornament where indicated on graph.

6 Slide last few pages of memo pad inside pocket.

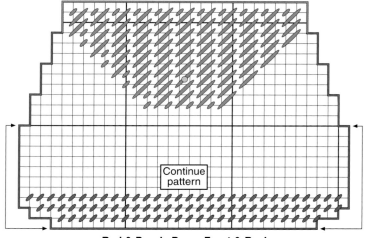

Red & Purple Purse Front & Back
31 holes x 22 holes
Cut 2
Stitch front as graphed
Stitch back entirely with
Christmas red Continental Stitches

Red & Purple Purse Inside Pocket
31 holes x 10 holes
Cut 1
Do not stitch

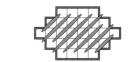

Red & Purple Purse Ornament
8 holes x 5 holes
Cut 1

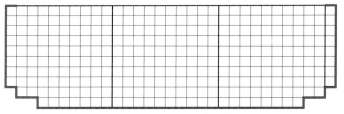

Red & Purple Purse Top
23 holes x 3 holes
Cut 1

COLOR KEY		
Yards	**Plastic Canvas Yarn**	
16 (14.7m)	■ Christmas red #01	
9 (8.3m)	■ Bright purple #64	
	○ Attach handle	
	● Attach ornament	
Color numbers given are for Uniek		
Needloft plastic canvas yarn.		

Red Hat Purse

Size: 6⅛ inches W x 3⅞ inches H x ¾ inch D
(15.6cm x 9.8cm x 1.9cm), excluding handle
and flower

Skill Level: Beginner

Materials

❏ ½ sheet 7-count plastic canvas
❏ Assorted beads from Blue Moon Beads
Lampworked Glass Bead Mix Red #47054

Stitching Step by Step

1 Cut plastic canvas according to graphs.

2 Stitch and Overcast flower following graph. Stitch front, back and top. Do not stitch inside pocket.

3 Using red, Whipstitch front and back to top.

4 Place inside pocket on wrong side of back where indicated with brackets. Using red and bright purple, Overcast around edges of assembled hat purse, Whipstitching pocket in place along side and bottom edges of back while Overcasting.

5 Following general instructions, assemble handle. Glue flower to front where indicated on graph.

6 Slide last few pages of memo pad inside pocket.

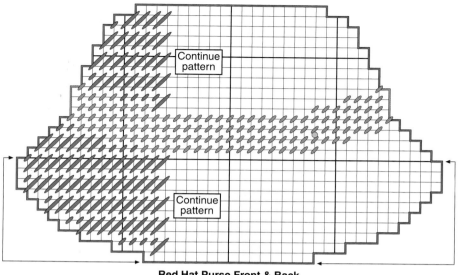

Red Hat Purse Front & Back
40 holes x 25 holes
Cut 2

Continue pattern

Continue pattern

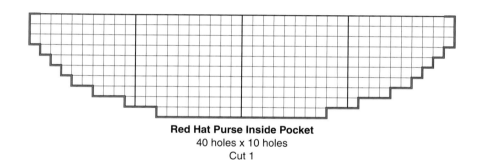

Red Hat Purse Inside Pocket
40 holes x 10 holes
Cut 1
Do not stitch

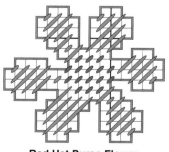

Red Hat Purse Flower
15 holes x 13 holes
Cut 1

COLOR KEY	
Yards	**Plastic Canvas Yarn**
20 (18.3m)	▪ Red #01
9 (8.3m)	▨ Bright purple #64
	○ Attach handle
	● Attach flower

Color numbers given are for Uniek Needloft plastic canvas yarn.

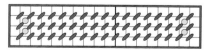

Red Hat Purse Top
18 holes x 4 holes
Cut 1

306 E. Parr Road
Berne, IN 46711
www.NeedlecraftShop.com
© 2005 The Needlecraft Shop

The full line of The Needlecraft Shop
products is carried by Annie's Attic catalog.
TOLL-FREE ORDER LINE
or to request a free catalog
(800) 582-6643
Customer Service
(800) 449-0440
Fax (800) 882-6643
Visit www.AnniesAttic.com

ISBN: 1-57367-185-1

All rights reserved.

Printed in USA

1 2 3 4 5 6 7 8 9

Shopping for Supplies

For supplies, first shop your local craft
and needlework stores. Some supplies
may be found in fabric, hardware and
discount stores. If you are unable to find
the supplies you need, please call Annie's
Attic at (800) 259-4000 for a free catalog
that sells plastic canvas supplies.

Getting Started

Before You Cut

Buy one brand of canvas for each entire project, as brands can dif-
fer slightly in the distance between bars. Count holes carefully from the
graph before you cut, using the bolder lines that show each 10 holes.
These 10-mesh lines begin in the lower left corner of each graph to make
counting easier. Mark canvas before cutting, then remove all marks completely before stitching. If the piece is cut in a rectangular or square shape
and is either not worked, or worked with only one color and one type of
stitch, we do not include the graph in the pattern. Instead, we give the
cutting and stitching instructions in the general instructions or with the
individual project instructions.

Covering the Canvas

Bring needle up from back of work, leaving a short length of yarn on
back of canvas; work over short length to secure. To end a thread, weave
needle and thread through the wrong side of your last few stitches; clip.
Follow the numbers on the tiny graphs beside each stitch illustration; bring
your needle up from the back of the work on odd numbers and down through
the front of the work on even numbers. Work embroidery stitches last, after
the canvas has been completely covered by the needlepoint stitches.

Basic Stitches

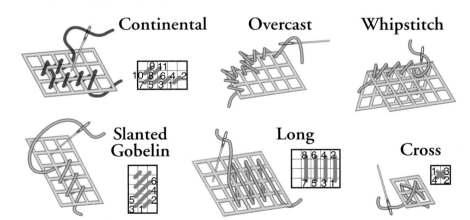

Embroidery Stitches

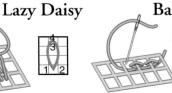

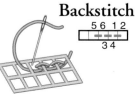

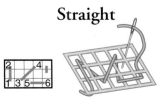

METRIC KEY:
millimeters = (mm)
centimeters = (cm)
meters = (m)
grams = (g)